Start to Finish
Second Series
Everyday Products

From Iron to Car

SHANNON ZEMLICKA

LERNER PUBLICATIONS COMPANY · Minneapolis

TABLE OF Contents

Lerner Publications Company
A division of Lerner Publishing Group, Inc.
241 First Avenue North
Minneapolis, MN 55401 U.S.A.

Website address: www.lernerbooks.com

Photo Acknowledgments

The images in this book are used with the permission of:
© iStockphoto.com/FokinOl, p. 1; © Transtock/SuperStock,
p. 3; © Nordic Photos/SuperStock, p. 5; © Sean Gallup/
Getty Images, p. 7; © James Hardy/PhotoAlto Agency
RF Collections/Getty Images, p. 9; © iStockphoto.com/
ricardoazoury, p. 11; © Bloomberg via Getty Images, p. 13;
© Stock Connection/SuperStock, p. 15; © SuperStock/
SuperStock, p. 17; © iStockphoto.com/FabioFilzi, p. 19;
© Bernhard Classen/Alamy, p. 20; © iStockphoto.com/
Pgiam, p. 23.

Front cover: © Mark Elias/Bloomberg via Getty Images.

Main body text set in Arta Std Book 20/26.
Typeface provided by International Typeface Corp.

Library of Congress Cataloging-in-Publication Data

Knudsen, Shannon, 1971–
    From iron to car / by Shannon Zemlicka.
        p.   cm. — (Start to finish, second series.
    Everyday products)
    Audience: Grades K to 3.
    Includes index.
    ISBN 978–0–7613–9182–1 (lib. bdg. : alk. paper)
    1. Automobiles—Design and construction—
Juvenile literature. 2. Automobiles—Materials—
Juvenile literature. 3. Steel-works—Juvenile literature.
I. Title.
TL240.K56 2013
629.2'3—dc23   2012007916

Manufactured in the United States of America
1 – MG – 12/31/12

Cars go fast and far.

How are they made?

Machines dig up iron ore.

A car starts as a metal called iron. Iron comes from iron ore. Iron ore is a mixture of iron and other metals or rocks. Big machines dig up iron ore from underground.

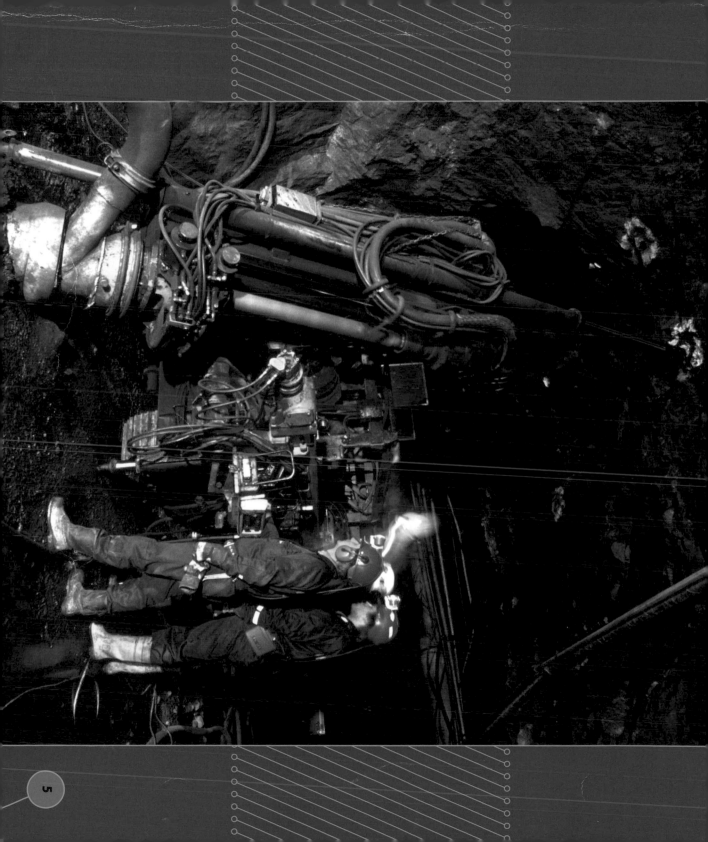

The iron ore is heated.

The iron ore is mixed with a rock called limestone. Burned charcoal is added. The mixture is heated. The iron melts into a thick liquid. Parts of the ore that are not iron float to the top. Workers remove these parts. Only iron is left.

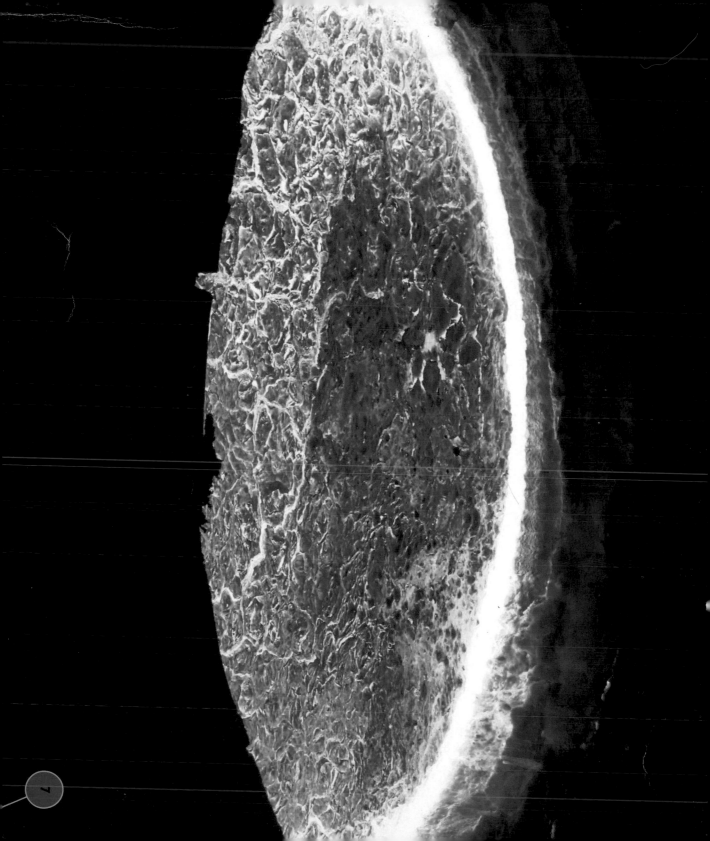

The iron is made into steel.

Pieces of steel are added to the iron. Steel is a kind of metal. It is stronger than iron. The iron and steel are melted together to make liquid steel.

The steel is shaped.

The liquid steel is poured into a machine that shapes it. Cold water cools the steel. It hardens. Then the steel is heated again. Huge rollers press the steel into strong, thin sheets.

Machines cut car parts.

Trains take the steel to a car **factory**. A factory is a place where things are made. Machines cut the steel sheets into doors, a hood, a trunk, and other car parts.

Machines put the parts together.

Machines use heat to melt the edges of the parts together. The parts cool and harden into one piece. This piece is the car's **body**.

The body is painted.

Machines cover the body with paint.

Paint protects the body and makes it look shiny. This body has been painted red.

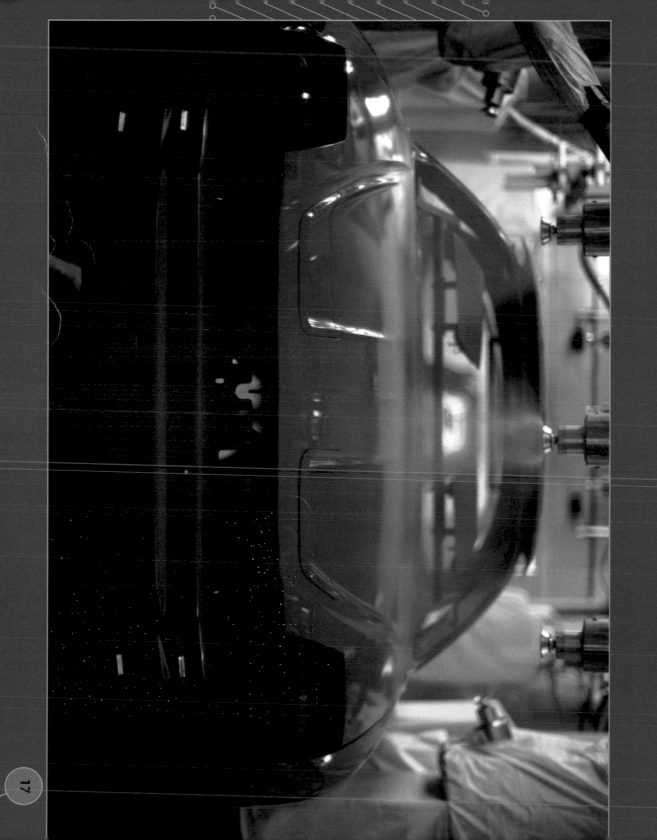

A machine cuts a frame.

A machine cuts a frame from sheets of steel. A frame is like a car's skeleton. An engine is attached to give the car power. Wheels are added.

The body is put on the frame.

Machines help put the body and frame together. Seats, windows, a steering wheel, and many other parts make the car complete.

Vroom, vroom!

The new cars are ready for the road!

They have gone from iron to car.

Glossary

body (BAH-dee): the outside shell of a car

factory (FAK-tur-ee): a place where things are made

frame (FRAYM): the part of a car that holds wheels and an engine

iron ore (EYE-uhrn OHR): a mixture of iron and rocks or metals

steel (STEEL): a metal that contains iron but is stronger

LERNER SOURCE

Expand learning beyond the printed book. Download free, complementary educational resources for this book from our website, www.lernersource.com.